TEC

Count On It!
Five

¡Cuenta con ello!
Cinco

Dana Meachen Rau

Marshall Cavendish
Benchmark
New York

Five fingers.

---❖---

Cinco dedos de la mano.

Five toes.

＊

Cinco dedos del pie.

Five sea shells.

❖

Cinco conchas
de mar.

Five rows.

———❖———

Cinco filas.

Five dogs.

———❖———

Cinco perros.

Five toys.

❖

Cinco juguetes.

Five candles.

❖

Cinco velas.

Five boys.

❖

Cinco niños.

Five!

❖

¡Cinco!

Words We Know
Palabras conocidas

boys
niños

candles
velas

dogs
perros

fingers
dedos de la mano

20

rows
filas

sea shells
conchas de mar

toes
dedos del pie

toys
juguetes

21

Index

Índice

About the Author

Dana Meachen Rau is the author of many other titles in the Bookworms series, as well as other nonfiction and early reader books. She lives in Burlington, Connecticut, with her husband and two children.

Datos biográficos de la autora

Dana Meachen Rau es la autora de muchos libros de la serie Bookworms y de otros libros de no ficción y de lectura inicial. Vive en Burlington, Connecticut, con su esposo y dos hijos.

With thanks to the Reading Consultants:

Nanci Vargus, Ed.D., is an Assistant Professor of Elementary Education at the University of Indianapolis.

Beth Walker Gambro is an Adjunct Professor at the University of St. Francis in Joliet, Illinois.

Agradecemos a las asesoras de lectura:

Nanci Vargus, Dra. en Ed. y profesora auxiliar de Educación Primaria en la Universidad de Indianápolis.

Beth Walker Gambro, profesora adjunta en la Universidad de St. Francis en Joliet, Illinois.

Marshall Cavendish Benchmark
99 White Plains Road
Tarrytown, New York 10591
www.marshallcavendish.us

Text copyright © 2009 by Marshall Cavendish Corporation

Library of Congress Cataloging-in-Publication Data

Rau, Dana Meachen, 1971–
[Five. Spanish & English]
Five / by Dana Meachen Rau = Cinco / por Dana Meachen Rau.
p. cm. – (Bookworms. Count on it! = ¡Cuenta con ello!)
Includes index.
ISBN 978-0-7614-3477-1 (bilingual ed.) – ISBN 978-0-7614-3449-8 (Spanish ed.)
ISBN 978-0-7614-2970-8 (English ed.)
1. Five (The number)–Juvenile literature. 2. Number concept–Juvenile literature.
I. Title. II. Title: Cinco.
QA141.3.R27518 2009
513.2'11–dc22
2008017247

Editor: Christina Gardeski
Publisher: Michelle Bisson
Designer: Virginia Pope
Art Director: Anahid Hamparian

Spanish Translation and Text Composition by Victory Productions, Inc.
www.victoryprd.com

Photo Research by Anne Burns Images

The photographs in this book are used with permission and through the courtesy of:
SuperStock: pp.1, 17, 20TL Digital Vision; pp. 7, 21TR age fotostock; pp. 11, 20BL GoGo Images; pp. 13, 21BR doll, top, duck Stockbyte; pp. 13, 21BR truck, boat Stockdisc. Corbis: pp. 3, 20BR Sean Justice; pp. 5, 21BL Mika/zefa; pp. 9, 21TL Simon Jarratt; pp. 15, 20TR JLP/Jose L. Pelaez; p. 19 Jeremy Hardie/zefa.

Printed in Malaysia
1 3 5 6 4 2